Where in the World Can I . . .

SEE A SEA MONSTER?

Where in the World Can I . . .

SEE A SEA MONSTER?

WORLD BOOK

www.worldbook.com

World Book, Inc.
180 North LaSalle Street, Suite 900
Chicago, Illinois 60601
USA

For information about other World Book publications, visit our website at **www.worldbook.com** or call **1-800-WORLDBK (967-5325).**

For information about sales to schools and libraries, call 1-800-975-3250 (United States), or 1-800-837-5365 (Canada).

Library of Congress Cataloging-in-Publication Data for this volume has been applied for.

Where in the World Can I...
ISBN: 978-0-7166-5251-9 (set, hc.)

See a Sea Monster?
ISBN: 978-0-7166-5254-0 (hc.)
ISBN: 978-0-7166-5266-3 (pf.)

Also available as:
ISBN: 978-0-7166-5260-1 (e-book)

STAFF

Acknowledgments
Writer: Cynthia O'Brien

Produced by
Focus Strategic Communications Inc.

TABLE OF CONTENTS

WHAT IS A SEA MONSTER?

You have probably seen pictures of sea monsters in books and movies. But did you know that many of these fantastic creatures are based on some amazing real-life animals?

No one knows exactly how many different creatures live in the ocean. There may be millions! The world's oceans are so vast and deep that more than 80 percent has never been explored or seen by humans. *Marine biologists* are scientists who study ocean life. So far, they have named over 200,000 ocean species, and they discover more all the time.

Marine biologists have helped identify some of the real creatures behind sea monster stories. Such animals as whales, oarfish, and the giant squid looked so huge and strange that they terrified early sailors. Even gentle manatees were thought to be *mermaids* luring sailors into the sea to drown. Mermaids are imaginary beings that are half human and half fish. Let's find out how all these sea monster stories started and where you can find sea monsters today.

In ancient times, people explained the world and its mysteries through stories called *myths*. Greek myths included a sea monster called Cetus. Later, Middle Eastern myths featured a monster called Leviathan. Both are whalelike creatures that were probably based on real whales.

Other mythical characters may be based on *prehistoric animals* (animals that existed more than 5,500 years ago). The stories may have started when ancient people uncovered *fossils* of some prehistoric sea creatures. Fossils are the remains of animals or plants that lived thousands or millions of years ago. Prehistoric sea creatures include such large reptiles as plesiosaurs *(PLEE see uh sawrz)* and giant mosasaurs *(MOH suh sawrz).*

Prehistoric sea monsters became *extinct* (died out) millions of years ago. But in 1977, Japanese fishermen caught a dead, large, and odd-looking animal in their net. It had a very long neck and tail, just like a *plesiosaur*. The fishermen took pictures and took a part of the animal's fin before throwing the body back into the sea. Today, most scientists think this strange animal was a shark, but no one knows for sure.

Many people's ideas about ocean life used to come from stories that sailors told. The stories spread, and most people believed the seas were full of strange and dangerous creatures. In the 1500's, Olaus Magnus created a colorful map of the land and seas of Scandinavia, in Northern Europe. He drew sea monsters in all the open seas. Magnus's descriptions and drawings were accepted and copied for many years.

Some imaginary sea creatures were described as sea serpents. These gigantic, snakelike fish have appeared in myths and stories from ancient times. People thought these creatures could snatch sailors from their boats and topple large ships into the ocean. In fact, these serpents were probably oarfish.

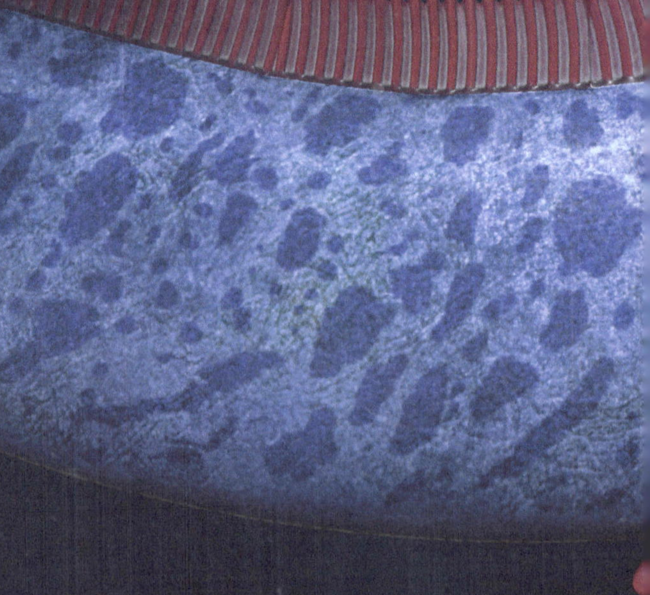

Oarfish are the largest bony fish in the world. Most measure up to 35 feet (11 meters) long, but some have grown to 55 feet (17 meters). That is more than half the length of a basketball court! Even though they are enormous, oarfish are not dangerous to people. They live deep in the ocean and eat tiny creatures called *krill*. Oarfish rarely come to the surface.

One of the sea creatures that frightened people the most was the kraken *(KRAH kuhn)*. According to Norse *folklore* (stories handed down through time), the kraken terrorized the seas around Scandinavia. The stories described the kraken as a mammoth sea creature with many long arms and *tentacles* (flexible arms of animals like the octopus). Also, it was so big it could eat whales and smash the largest ships. Traditional tales from around the world featured a similar monster.

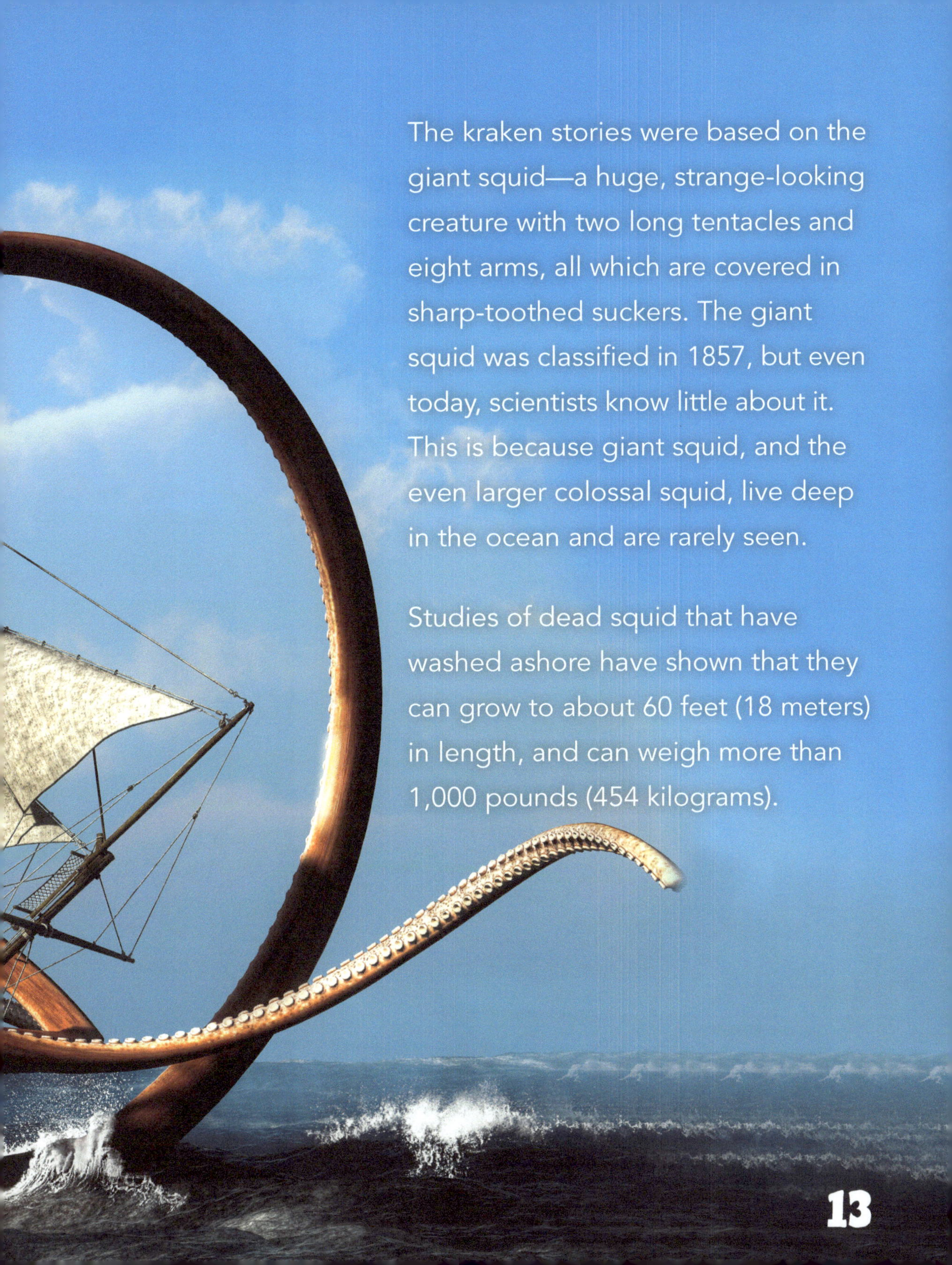

The kraken stories were based on the giant squid—a huge, strange-looking creature with two long tentacles and eight arms, all which are covered in sharp-toothed suckers. The giant squid was classified in 1857, but even today, scientists know little about it. This is because giant squid, and the even larger colossal squid, live deep in the ocean and are rarely seen.

Studies of dead squid that have washed ashore have shown that they can grow to about 60 feet (18 meters) in length, and can weigh more than 1,000 pounds (454 kilograms).

Do monsters live in lakes, too? Some people think so. Probably the most famous of these is Scotland's Loch Ness Monster, or Nessie. Others include Ogopogo and Champ. Ogopogo supposedly lurks in Okanagan Lake, British Columbia, Canada. Champ is a legendary serpent of Lake Champlain, which lies between New York and Vermont, and extends into southwest Québec, Canada.

Stories about lake serpents go back many years. Over generations, people in Scotland handed down tales of Nessie. But the monsters became world famous in 1934, after a doctor claimed he had taken its photograph. The picture turned out to be a *hoax* (a trick meant to fool people).

In North America, the Salish (people native to Western Canada) told stories of N'ha-a-itk, a sea serpent in Okanagan Lake. Later, European settlers called the creature Ogopogo. Many people have reported seeing Ogopogo, but there is no real proof that it exists. The same is true for Champ. Abenaki people who lived around Lake Champlain told stories about a lake serpent called Gitaskog. In fact, Gitaskog, or Champ, is likely a large fish called a sturgeon.

Feeling brave? Turn the page to start exploring where in the world you can find sea monsters!

GEORGIA AQUARIUM

A visit to an *aquarium* is a great way to look at sea monsters up close. Aquariums are small or large tanks filled with water where fish and other marine animals can live. The Georgia Aquarium in Atlanta, Georgia, is one of the largest in the world. Here you can find sea monsters like sharks and manta rays. You can also visit friendly beluga whales, bottlenose dolphins, and sea otters. If you ever wondered what sea creatures do at night, you can have a sleepover at the aquarium.

Sea monster hunters have loads to explore at the aquarium's exhibits and visitor experiences. The massive Ocean Voyager tank holds 6.3 million gallons (24 million liters) of water. It is full of sea life, including the largest ocean fish in the world, the whale shark. The Ocean Voyager tank features a glass tunnel you can walk through. See what you can spot up above and all around you. Some of the creatures might come up to the glass to say hello!

Whale sharks are the Georgia Aquarium star residents. The aquarium is the only one outside of Asia to house this species. These sea creatures are huge! The biggest ever recorded was almost 62 feet (19 meters) long—a little longer than a bowling lane.

Whale sharks may look scary, but they do not want to attack people. They eat *zooplankton*, the tiniest creatures in the ocean.

If you are 12 years or older and have an adult with you, you can meet whale sharks in a "Journey with the Gentle Giants." Put on a wet suit and grab a snorkel! A trainer will take you into the Ocean Voyagers tank for a 30-minute swim among whale sharks, friendly manta rays, and other fish.

Look closely—each whale shark has its own spot pattern. If you have a diving certificate, you can go on a deep, 30-minute dive using SCUBA equipment. Wave to the people in the viewing gallery as you pass by.

To see other sea monsters up close, Georgia Aquarium offers an amazing Shark Cave Dive. This awesome experience puts you in the middle of a 20-foot- (6-meter-) deep shark habitat. Sharks! Predators of the Deep has a massive 185-foot- (56-meter-) long glass viewing gallery. Divers stay safe inside a shark-proof cage while great hammerheads, tiger sharks, silky sharks, and more swim around.

Great hammerheads are easy to spot with their wide, flat heads. Their eyes are located at either end of their rectangular heads. Hammerheads hunt rays, including poisonous stingrays. Tiger sharks get their name from the stripes across their bodies. These sharks feed on rays, but also on many other kinds of animals, including bony fish and reptiles.

People used to be very afraid of manta rays, telling stories about how they attacked ships and ate sailors. In fact, these sea monsters are very gentle and very curious about people. In the wild, they are at risk from humans who hunt them or catch them in their fishing nets.

Rays have wide, flat bodies and are related to sharks. There are hundreds of different kinds of rays. Stingrays have a poisonous barb on their tails, which can be dangerous to people. Manta rays do not have this barb. The manta ray is the biggest of all the rays. The giant manta ray has a wingspan of 29 feet (9 meters).

In a shallow section of the shark exhibit, you can interact with sharks and even pet manta rays. To take part in this activity, you must be 48 inches (1.2 meters) tall. If you are younger than 16 years in age, you must have an adult with you. This program includes an information session all about sharks.

CRYSTAL RIVER NATIONAL WILDLIFE REFUGE, FLORIDA

When Christopher Columbus sailed into the Caribbean Sea in 1492, he thought he spotted some mermaids. Early sailors like Columbus believed these magical creatures caused ships to run aground and lured sailors into the water to drown. Now we know that Columbus probably saw manatees.

Every year, from mid-November to late March, hundreds of West Indian manatees gather in the warm waters of Crystal River, on the west coast of Florida. Crystal River is north of Tampa. Crystal River National Wildlife Refuge is one of the best places to visit the manatees in their winter home.

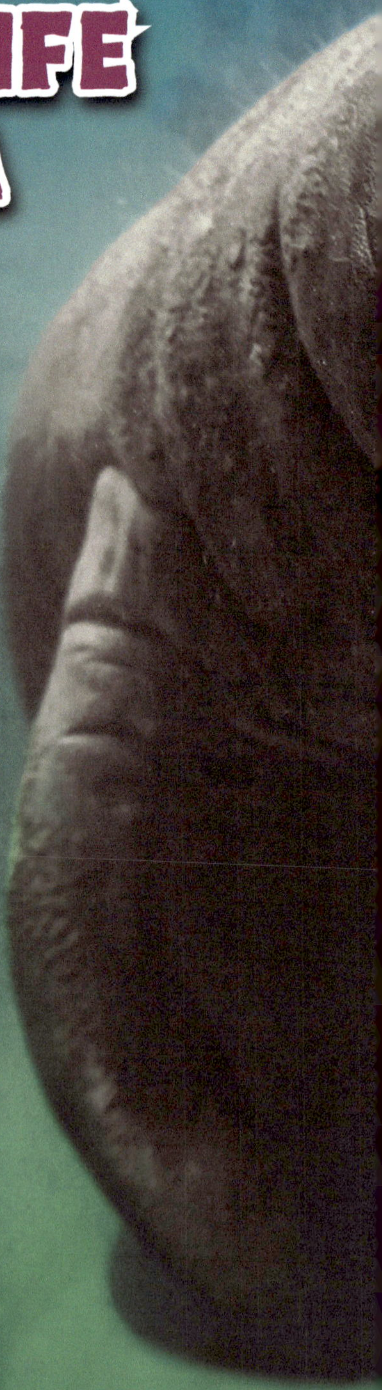

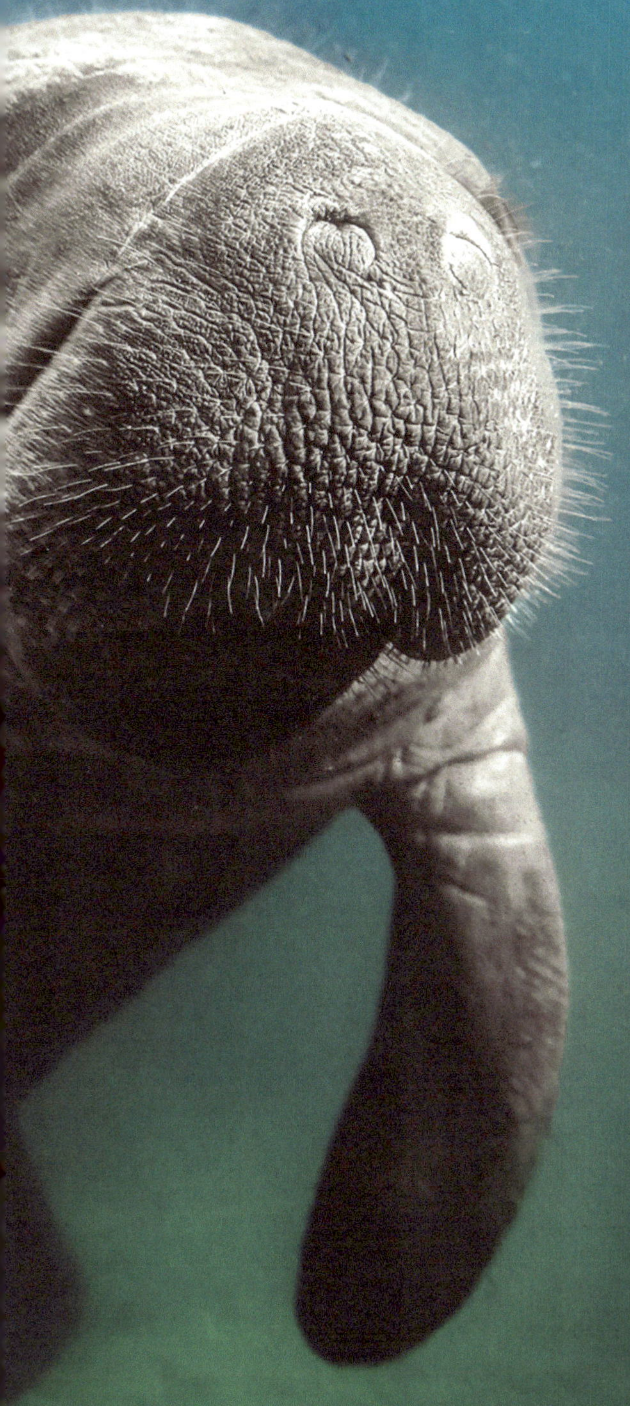

A manatee is a large *marine mammal* that weighs about 1,000 pounds (454 kilograms). Like other mammals, mother manatees nurse their young. Manatees live in the sea but must come to the surface to breathe air. They are *herbivores* (animals that eat plants) and move slowly through the water.

Manatees are *threatened* animals, which means that they need to be protected to survive. It is illegal to hunt them now, but many still die in accidents with boats or from loss of *habitat* (where they normally live).

When you visit the Crystal River area, there are many opportunities to see and learn about the manatees. You can take out a canoe or go on a tour boat. There are many viewing platforms, such as boardwalks, where you can peek at the manatees from above.

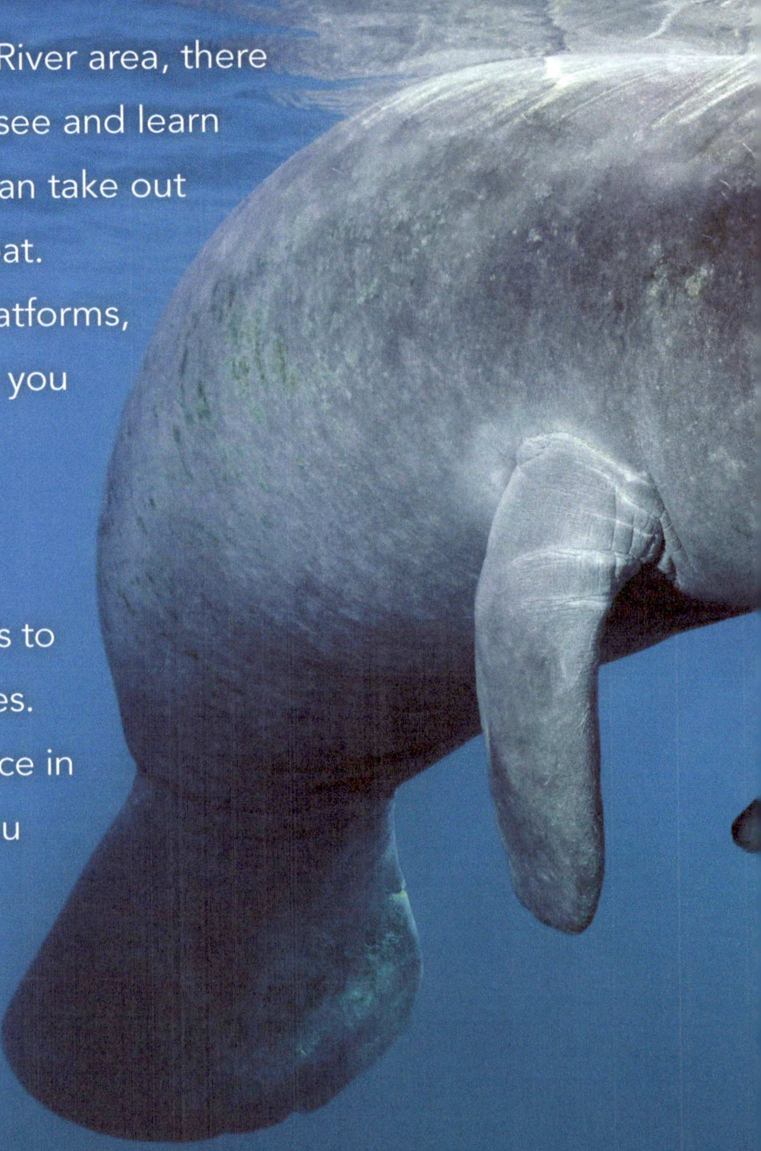

A truly special experience is to go swimming with manatees. Crystal River is the only place in the United States where you can do this legally. Here, you will see manatees in their natural habitat, so you should be careful not to bother them. Before you go swimming or boating, experienced guides will tell you all about manatees and the rules you should follow while you are around them. These rules help to keep both the manatees—and you—safe.

Do look at manatees, but do not try to chase, feed, or pet them. Never try to separate a baby manatee from its mother. Also, do not splash around or make a lot of noise that will disturb the manatees. If you are manatee-watching from a boat, you must be extra careful. Manatees may not notice the boat approaching, so boaters should always proceed with caution. It is also important that you never go over a manatee swimming underneath or it might become injured.

MONTEREY BAY AQUARIUM

Monterey, California, is a city in the western United States, on the edge of the Pacific Ocean. The Monterey Bay Aquarium overlooks the bay, which is part of a protected area of water called the Monterey Bay National Marine Sanctuary. After you visit the aquarium, you can also take time to explore the different parts of the sanctuary.

The Monterey Bay Aquarium has over 200 exhibits to discover. Some of the main ones include the Open Sea Exhibit and the Ocean's Edge galleries. These exhibits highlight some of the sea monsters and other creatures that are at home in Monterey Bay.

Since it opened in 1984, the aquarium has been a window to the Pacific Ocean's amazing wildlife. The scientists at the aquarium are dedicated to helping *conserve* (protect) the habitat and its animals. It is the only aquarium in the world to have exhibited, protected, and then released great white sharks.

The Open Sea Exhibit is the largest in the aquarium. Through its 90-foot- (27-meter-) long window, you can view creatures like the scalloped hammerhead shark, green turtle, jellyfish, and stingray.

The Eastern Pacific scalloped hammerhead is an *endangered* species. This means it is at risk of dying out. These large sharks can reach up to 11 feet (3.4 meters) in length.

In the same exhibit, green turtles move around looking for seagrasses to munch on. This favorite food turns the turtle's fat green. Green turtles are one of the world's largest sea turtles and can weigh up to 400 pounds (181 kilograms). Like the hammerhead, species of green turtle are either endangered or threatened.

Weird and remarkable creatures *inhabit* (live in) the aquarium's Kelp Forest. It is 28 feet (8.5 meters) high and one of the tallest exhibits of its kind. Kelp is a type of seaweed that grows fast and large, and can be densely packed. It grows in shallow coastal waters. The thick groups of kelp create a kind of underwater forest. In the wild, a wide variety of marine animals use kelp for shelter, food, and protection from *predators* (hunters).

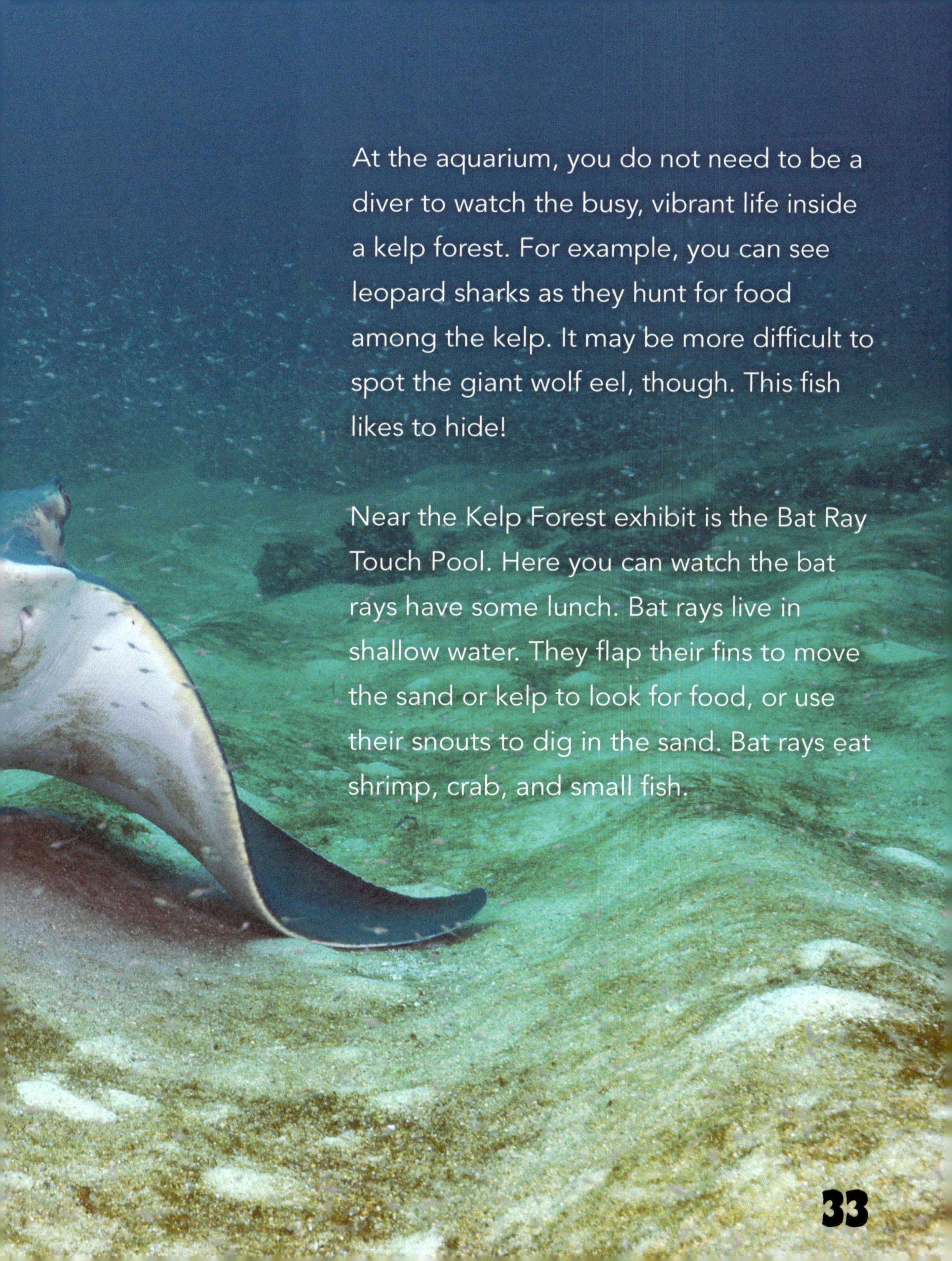

At the aquarium, you do not need to be a diver to watch the busy, vibrant life inside a kelp forest. For example, you can see leopard sharks as they hunt for food among the kelp. It may be more difficult to spot the giant wolf eel, though. This fish likes to hide!

Near the Kelp Forest exhibit is the Bat Ray Touch Pool. Here you can watch the bat rays have some lunch. Bat rays live in shallow water. They flap their fins to move the sand or kelp to look for food, or use their snouts to dig in the sand. Bat rays eat shrimp, crab, and small fish.

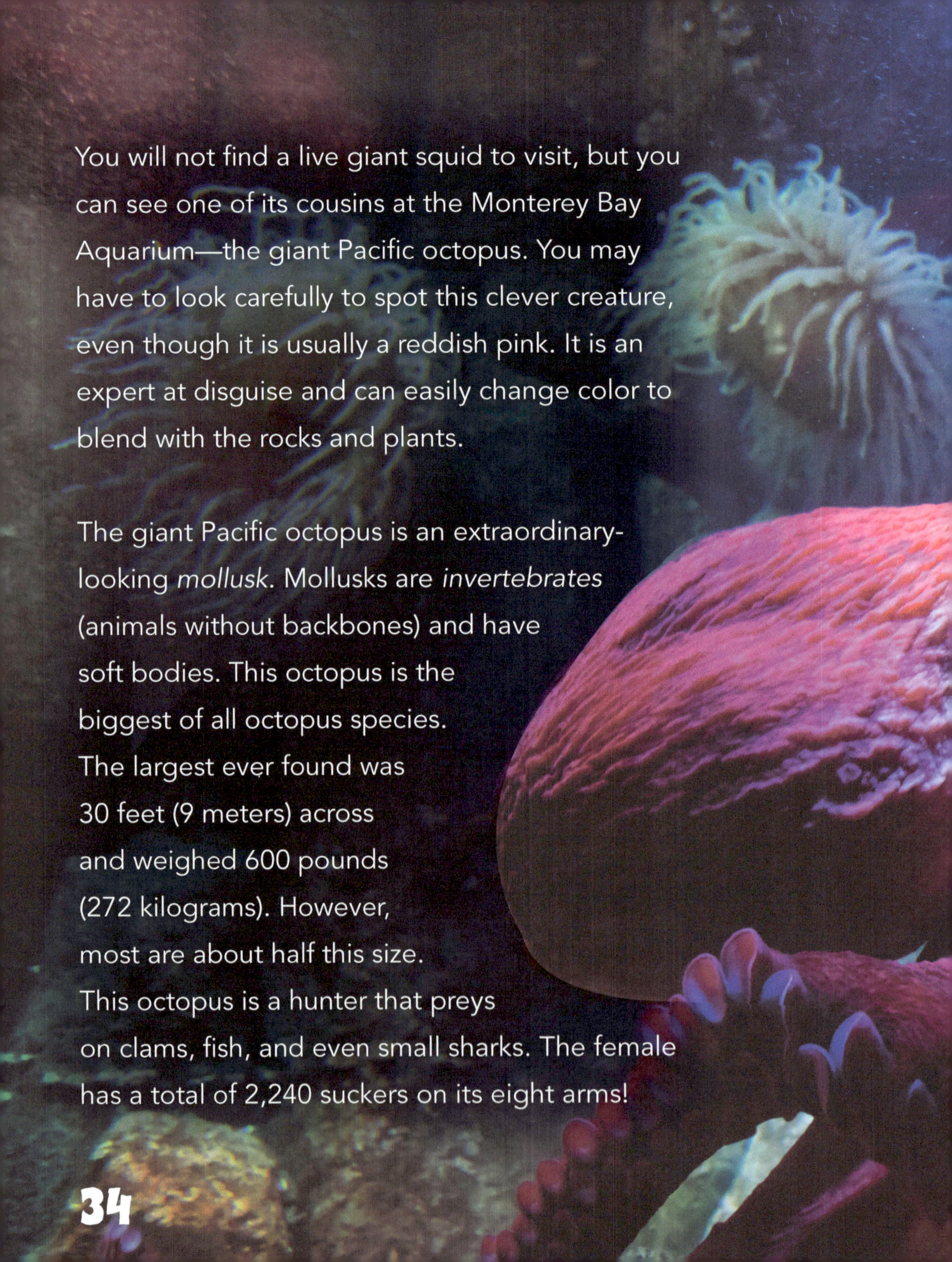

You will not find a live giant squid to visit, but you can see one of its cousins at the Monterey Bay Aquarium—the giant Pacific octopus. You may have to look carefully to spot this clever creature, even though it is usually a reddish pink. It is an expert at disguise and can easily change color to blend with the rocks and plants.

The giant Pacific octopus is an extraordinary-looking *mollusk*. Mollusks are *invertebrates* (animals without backbones) and have soft bodies. This octopus is the biggest of all octopus species. The largest ever found was 30 feet (9 meters) across and weighed 600 pounds (272 kilograms). However, most are about half this size. This octopus is a hunter that preys on clams, fish, and even small sharks. The female has a total of 2,240 suckers on its eight arms!

The giant Pacific octopus is a very clever animal. It has a large brain in its head and a small brain in each of its arms. It can open jars, solve maze puzzles, and recognize some of the workers at the aquarium.

The aquarium's location on Monterey Bay makes it the ideal place to see sea monsters and other ocean creatures in their natural habitat. The Life on the Bay exhibit includes a Marine Mammal Gallery where you can look up to see life-size models of a gray whale and an orca. Outside, at the Wildlife Viewing Station, you can see sea lions and seals near the rocky shore. Pick up a pair of the aquarium's binoculars to see what you can spot on the rocky shore or way out at sea.

If you are very lucky, you may spot a blue whale. This gigantic whale is the largest animal on Earth. It can grow to 100 feet (30 meters) long and weigh up to 200 tons (181 metric tons). No wonder people used to think it was a sea monster! Other whales also visit Monterey Bay. You may see a *pod* (group) of orcas. The orca is a dolphin, but it is sometimes called the killer whale for its ferocious hunting skills. Orcas are easy to spot with their black and white bodies. Look out for other dolphins and porpoises, too.

HÚSAVÍK, ICELAND

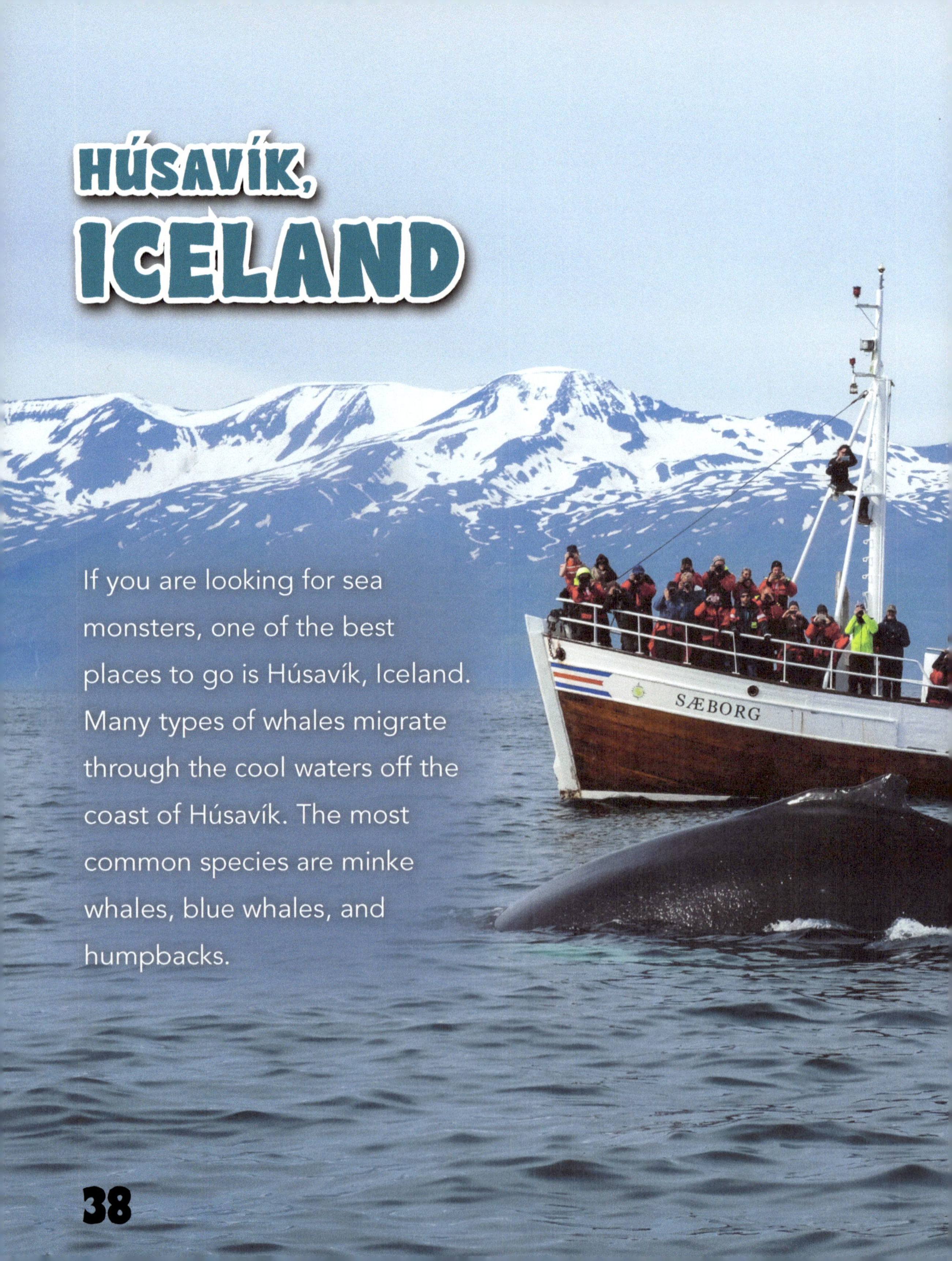

If you are looking for sea monsters, one of the best places to go is Húsavík, Iceland. Many types of whales migrate through the cool waters off the coast of Húsavík. The most common species are minke whales, blue whales, and humpbacks.

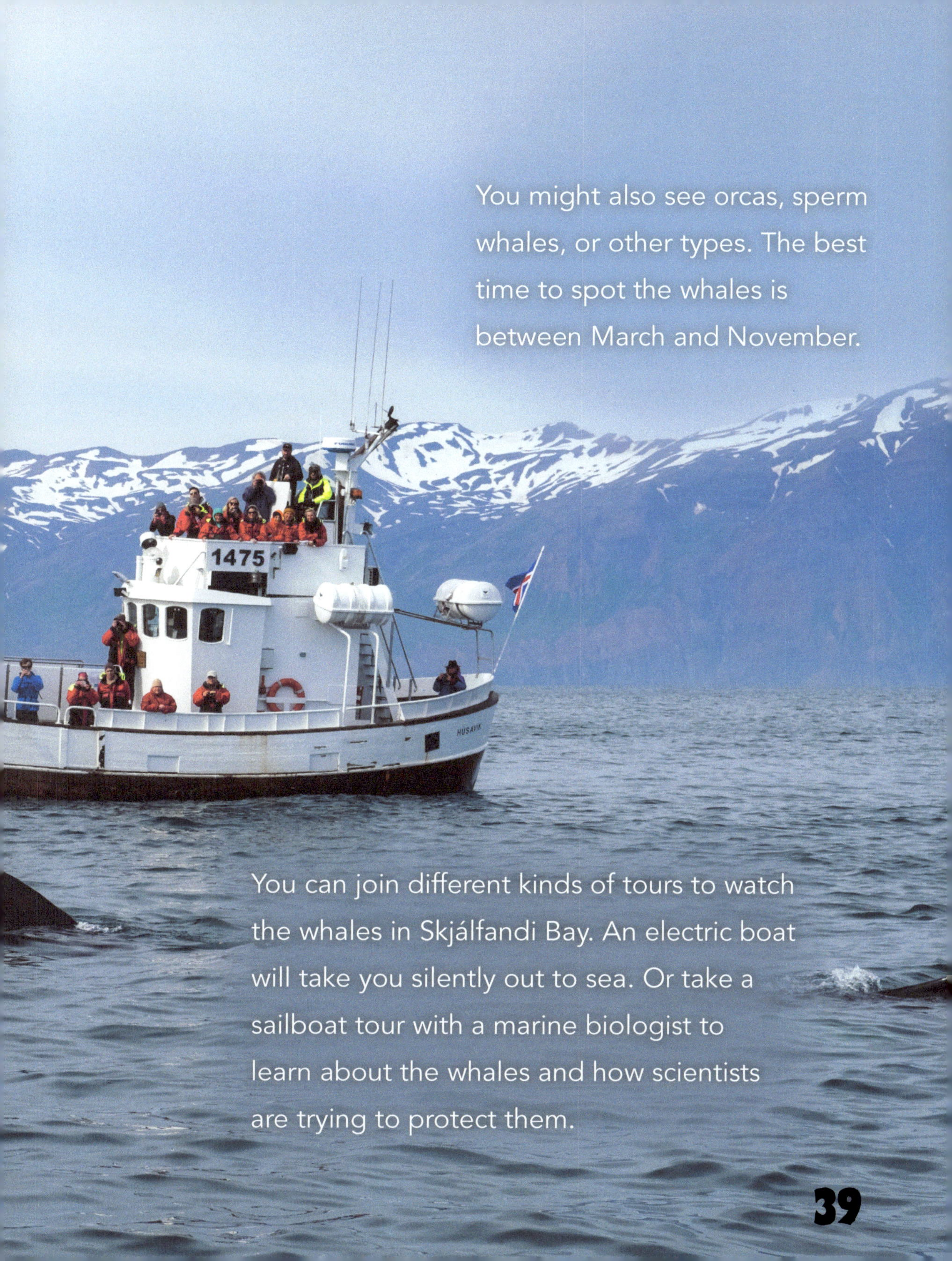

You might also see orcas, sperm whales, or other types. The best time to spot the whales is between March and November.

You can join different kinds of tours to watch the whales in Skjálfandi Bay. An electric boat will take you silently out to sea. Or take a sailboat tour with a marine biologist to learn about the whales and how scientists are trying to protect them.

Humpbacks travel and congregate in pods, and they are very talented water acrobats. This makes them a lot of fun to watch. Long ago, however, people may have thought these sea monsters were planning to attack!

Humpbacks perform spectacular *breaches*. This is when a whale leaps upward out of the water. It uses its powerful tail to push itself out of the water, coming back with a huge splash. Humpbacks may do this to communicate with other whales or even just for fun. They also seem to communicate with each other by slapping their fins on the water.

Humpbacks have other amazing behaviors to watch. Spyhopping is when the whale pokes its head out of the water to have a look around.

Bubble-net feeding is a group activity. The whales dive below the fish they want to eat, blowing bubbles as they spin and rise up. The bubbles create a kind of net that traps the fish, and the whales gulp them up as they come to the surface.

Before or after you go whale watching, you will not want to miss a trip to the Húsavík Whale Museum. The museum has over eight exhibition rooms, including one with information about whale behavior, habitat, and more. This room also explains how whales have *evolved* (changed over time).

To learn even more, watch *Whale Wisdom* in the screening room. This film explains how these clever marine animals communicate, hunt, and play.

The museum's "whale walk" gallery is a display of 11 huge whale skeletons. The largest is the skeleton of an 82-foot- (25-meter-) long blue whale. All these whales died of natural causes, except for the narwhal, which was gifted to the museum.

Narwhals live in cold Arctic waters and are nicknamed "unicorns of the sea." Like imaginary unicorns, male narwhals and a very few females have a long tooth that sticks straight out from their head, forming a tusk.

OTHER PLACES TO VISIT

There are many other places in the world to find sea monsters. Here are some of them:

Curaçao Sea Aquarium, Willemstad, Curaçao

You can feed the sharks and watch deep sea life without a snorkel. The aquarium has an open-water system that allows ocean water to flow through.

Kaikōura, New Zealand

Kaikōura is located on the east coast of New Zealand's South Island. Here, you can see sperm whales all year round.

Nausicaa, Boulogne-sur-Mer, France

One of the largest aquariums in Europe, Nausicaa is on the western coast of France. There are over 58,000 creatures to see, including sharks, giant manta rays, and more.

L'Oceanogràfic, Valencia, Spain

This huge aquarium is the largest in Europe and home to over 45,000 marine animals, including a family of beluga whales.

Okinawa Churaumi Aquarium, Motobu, Okinawa, Japan

This massive aquarium is part of Ocean Expo Park and is home to hundreds of different species of marine life, including whale sharks. The main tank holds almost 2 million gallons (7.5 million liters) of water.

S.E.A. Aquarium, Sentosa, Singapore

This is one of the world's largest aquariums, with more than 100,000 marine creatures, including 12 species of shark.

SEA LIFE Sydney Aquarium, Sydney, Australia

Visit a dugong and take a trip into the underwater Shark Valley Tunnel to see these amazing sea monsters up close.

The Azores, Portugal

This group of islands, called an archipelago, are in the North Atlantic Ocean off the coast of Portugal. Visitors experience some of the best whale watching in the world in the seas surrounding these islands. Sperm and pilot whales are seen often here. Many kinds of dolphins are common, too, including bottlenoses and Risso's dolphin.

Vancouver Aquarium, Vancouver, British Columbia, Canada

The aquarium includes a marine mammal rescue facility that saves sea lion pups, sea turtles, and more.

Vancouver Island, British Columbia, Canada

Thousands of whales migrate past the island's Pacific Ocean coast. Visitors will see gray whales, minke whales, and humpbacks. This whale watching center also has resident orcas. These are orcas that stay in the area all year round.

READING FOCUS

Text Structure is all about the way a text is organized. When we know the structure, we can focus more of our energy and attention on comprehending what we read.

This book uses a Description Text Structure. It describes a topic and its characteristics using details, adjectives, and a logical order. Description texts often use examples to show and explain the main idea or topic.

Description texts usually include a lot of interesting details. We can use a graphic organizer to help us keep track of the most important information.

Prove It!

Find at least 3 examples from the text that support the claim that this book uses a Description Text Structure.

1. This is a Bubble Diagram, a strong graphic organizer for Description texts. Visit **www.worldbook.com/resources** to download and print copies or create your own!
2. As you read and/or revisit the text, complete a Bubble Diagram for EACH section:
   - Georgia Aquarium
   - Crystal River National Wildlife Refuge, Florida
   - Monterey Bay Aquarium
   - Húsavík, Iceland
3. For each section, write the title in the center-most bubble. Next, add important details to the bubbles attached to that central, main idea. Remember, you do not have enough bubbles for *every* detail. Think critically to determine which details to include.

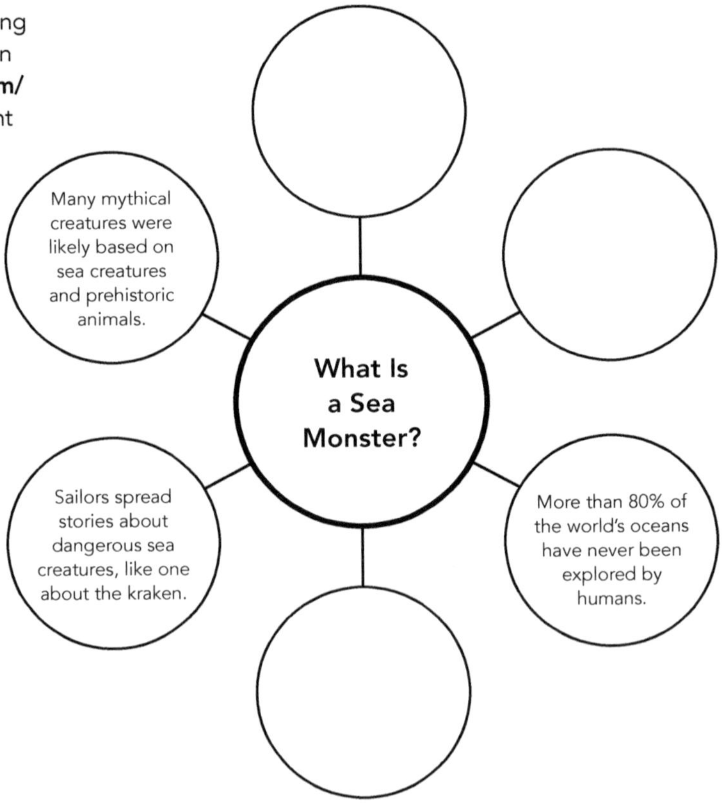

What other information about seeing sea monsters will you add to your Bubble Diagram?

WRITING FOCUS

What do YOU think?

In your opinion, which of the four spotlighted locations would be best for seeing sea monsters?

Review the notes you took on your Bubble Diagrams. Use evidence from the text, supported by logical reasoning, to answer the question. Your writing should include:

- A **hook** where you grab your readers' attention
- A **thesis statement** where you state your opinion
- At least 3 **reasons** why that is your opinion
- At least 3 **details** that support each reason

Use an Opinion Writing Graphic Organizer to sort through your thoughts before you write your response. Create your own or download and print a version from **www.worldbook.com/ resources.**

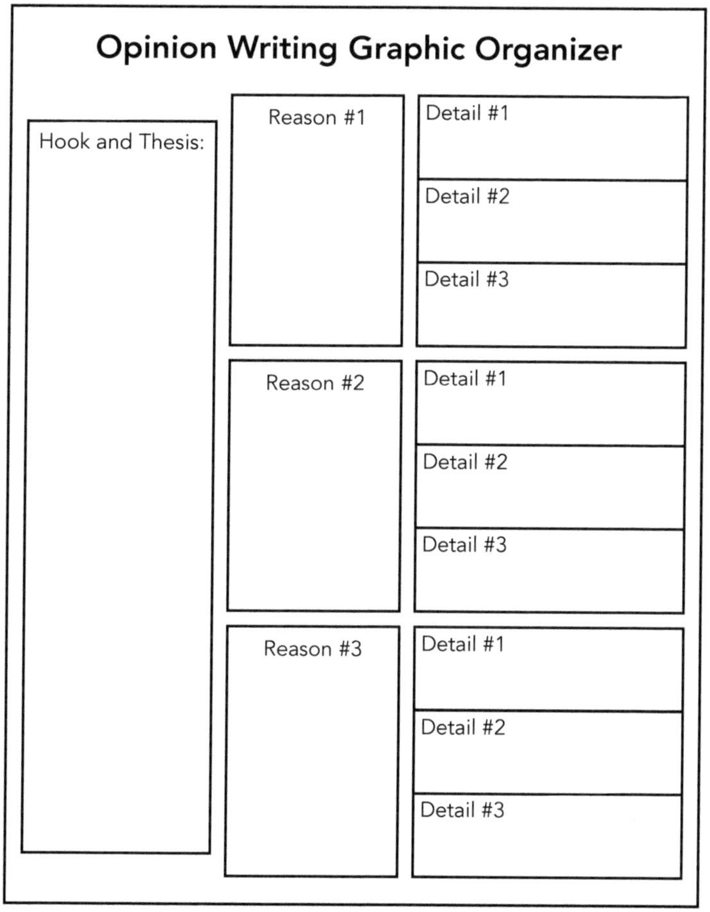

You might have noticed some words in this book written in *italics*. That means they are vocabulary terms! **Challenge yourself!** Can you include at least 5 of these words in your opinion writing?

INDEX

ACKNOWLEDGMENTS

Cover: © Obsidian Fantasy Studio, Shutterstock
TP: © Konstantin G, Shutterstock
6–7 © Michael Rosskothen, Shutterstock
8–9 © Daniel Eskridge, Shutterstock
10–11 © Whpics, dreamstime; © Dotted Yeti, Shutterstock
12–13 © Daniel Eskridge, Shutterstock
14–15 © imageBROKER/Roland Marske, Alamy; © Daniel Eskridge, Shutterstock
16–17 © Ravenash, Shutterstock
18–19 © Vlad G, Shutterstock
20–21 © Tomas Kotouc, Shutterstock; © HakBak, Shutterstock
22–23 © Venko, Shutterstock
24–25 © Jeff Stamer, Shutterstock
26–27 © imageBROKER/Norbert Probst, Alamy
28–29 © vanchai tan, Shutterstock
30–31 © Jamie Pham, Alamy
32–33 © photocritical, Shutterstock; © Reinhard Dirscherl, Alamy
34–35 © Mindy Lindford, dreamstime
36–37 © Chase Dekker, Shutterstock
38–39 © Remizov, Shutterstock
40–41 © Martin Prochazkacz, Shutterstock
42–43 © Dotted Yeti, Shutterstock; © Martin Mehes, Alamy
44–45 © Gregorio Koji, Shutterstock

www.ingramcontent.com/pod-product-compliance
Ingram Content Group UK Ltd.
Pitfield, Milton Keynes, MK11 3LW, UK
UKHW061028310726
14090UKWH00027B/354

* 9 7 8 0 7 1 6 6 5 2 6 6 3 *